THE BLACK BOOK

DEAN MEREDITH

Copyright © 2017 Dean Meredith

ISBN: 978-1-925590-63-0
Published by Vivid Publishing
A division of Fontaine Publishing Group
P.O. Box 948, Fremantle
Western Australia 6959
www.vividpublishing.com.au

Cataloguing-in-Publication data is available from the National Library of Australia

All rights reserved. No part of this publication may be reproduced, stored in a retrieval system or transmitted in any form or by any means, electronic, mechanical, photocopying, recording or otherwise, without the prior written permission of the copyright holder. The information, views, opinions and visuals expressed in this publication are solely those of the author(s) and do not necessarily reflect those of the publisher.

1ˢᵗ Night

I so still & quiet
Like soft little mousy
She so quirky
And listens through hair
He so funny
Like friendly Gonzo
She so brown
And mind like rainbow
He with time
Plays with money
She so tall
Lips like honey
She so nice
And melancholy
He like salt
She so Ernest
And him so proper
And he like grape
All so clever

23

They gave me days
They gave me 23
To live and breathe
And really see

They gave me days
They gave me 23
Days of calendars
And clocks

Twenty-three
Twenty-three

And after all
His miracles
He still believed
In twenty-three

Has he?
Smelled your fur?
Quite possibly
If it were only
Twenty-three

But it's all a big if
Whether or not
She's true
Twenty-three

I don't know
But twenty-three

One last hurrah
For twenty-three

A Dark Wind Blew

What was that?
The wind said
As it breathed
… Death
Into the room
And weaved
A withered foot
And limped
Candle lit
… Unholy
In the gloom
It said …
Rush away
Be gone
Be gone
And soon

A storm of thoughts
Thundered on
And rained …
Over the moon
Old dead wood
Creaked and moaned
Grinding teeth …
Through skin and bone
Blood sparks flew
From rusted nails
Windows shrieked
The banshee wailed
Beautifully done son
Beautifully done

The darkness ...
Will help you see

'A' Minor

My melancholy friend
A resinous bow
The queen bee
Covered in pollen
And her drones
All around her
The maiden hair
How the honey sticks
Her down between his legs
The long slow buzz
The back and forth
The strings
The neck
The body
The spike

Camel-Toe

Camel-toe
Oh camel-toe
How I love thee
Camel-toe

The way you come
The way you go
Camel-toe
Oh camel-toe

You only show
Your outer glow
When what's within
I'd rather know

Your hills and valleys
Down below
Your double you
That seam you sew

It's as though
Oh camel-toe
You're giving us
A private show

How I love thee
Camel-toe
The way you come
The way you go

Christmas Snacks

Yeah so cave and co
Bled their menace
Through my meat grinder
Brain on a hot salt
Rain dripping
Cloud covered
Liberating libatious
Beer soaked
Pizza perfect
Garlic fingered
Almost summer day
But I felt cool
Looked like a
Liquored up has-been
Throne back
From a barred room
Pathetic one hooker
Dance and I land
With a bounce
Like a fat king rat
All belly and whiskers
Tail in tact
Nose pointed
And a quirky
Little alley cat
Invites me home
To share her biscuits
She has me for dinner
I have her for dessert
Then she shows me
Her secret kitty stash

And she looks so cute
With those green almond eyes
And her I've got it walk
And her tail in the air
So I get down
And devour those bones
Sucking the marrow
Licking the best bits
Clean and dry
Then we pause
To develop our crazy smiles
And roll on our backs
And drift off like bats
As though it all was a
Dream of sorts
Where roles get blurred
And positions reversed
And it just don't matter
Who follows or leads
Coz that stuff just
Gets in the way
It's all about the music
And all about the song
And feeling
The words
They say

Crossing the Line

Oh that's quite a pair
Of legs you have there
You cross them so easily
Like two live wires
Positive and negative
Separate but connected
By a secret something
Surging from within

Dark Stranger

Hello mister
You ragged old thing
All ruffled feathers
And black sharpness
Menacing looks
Garbled cries
Misunderstood
But fascinating
Continually taunted
By small minds
Shadow puppets
Against the sun
You terrify
And enthral
With your mystery
Appear from nowhere
Eye us through
And then …
You're gone

Déjà Vu

Two men
Walk alone
At the same time
But years apart
Both look
To the past
Footsteps similar
But not the same
The sand knows them
An old sirocco
Pleads indifference
Just because it can
And history knows
Always remembers
It felt the footprints
Deep within
All so serious
Laughing
As they go

Dreaming of Happy

We're always sorry
After showing our worst
To the ones we adore
Who love us the most?
Taking us back
Again and again
Despite their best thoughts
Hearts bigger than forever
Innocent stray kittens
Full of soft hope
Blind as street lights
Searching for stars
Impossibly far
From homely drains
And thin spider friends
All dreaming of happy
But settling for tomorrow
One crazy moon
After another
Smiling at pain
Through rain soaked mud
Forgiving their brutes
Poor sweet brothers
Out to impress
Those fatherly ghosts
Blowing breathy fingers
Shaking one more game
Loaded dice spinning
Praying like hellfire
For him and for them
Rolling point on point

With crushed velvet slide
Until the flat stop
Of skid row bone
And their little heads
Closer than a family
Milk white together
Pink tongues lapping
Hungry as a wedding
Dancing just for fun
Taking us back
Again and again

Fathers' Day

All sunshine
And cum
Quiet
Like prison sex
Bicycles
Birds fly in
Noise
Fly out
Radio drone
Red faced
Computer
Dirty

Feral Moan

You put your scent on me
And I was yours
You waived your tail in the air
And skunked me

You scrambled my senses
Like a stealth bimbo
You carpet fucked me
And burned a stain

You screwed me up and in
Like a flashing bulb
And your dextrous fingers
Flicked my switch

Finer Things

Do you like the finer things?
Blue cheese
Green olives
Cum in your mouth
A cock up your ass
A fist in your cunt
A blindfold
And handcuffs
A hand on your throat
Do you appreciate the finer things?
French champagne
Russian caviar
Blue cheese
Licking shower walls
A diamond ring
Could it be zirconium?
Do you like the finer things?

Four Pirates

At the bar
Waiting to score
A little something
We pull a cone each
The other Steve
He was a jockey long ago
Face lined by life
Now that's a knife!
His young friend from jail
The Irishman on edge
Looking for a fight
He notices my shoes
Brand new Doc Martins
"They'll need Dubbin"
I wonder if he's carrying
A gun
Steve starts his chainsaw
No-one flinches

Getting Hard to Play

Just let me love you fuck you!
With an ironic dick & girly hands
I will have that reclusive tongue
And suck your piano fingers
Press those soft pink buttons
I'll lick you clean
And ignite your purr
You messed up feline
You cute hot tease
You invisible muse
Open close
Tempt me in
Avoid my lasers
And ban my ass
Weed me, wet me
Watch me grow

Hard Shoe

Mm ...
That sound ...
Of her long ... slow
... High heel toe
On the hard wood floor
On the other side
Of the thin green wall
With the smoky window
In the small dark room
With the lock on the door
Next to all the other
Small dark rooms
With thin green walls
And locks on the doors
And smoky windows
All with views to the stage
With her and those shoes
At the centre of attention
From the windows of the rooms
With the locks on the doors
And the thump of the music
And the pump of her shoes
As she struts around
On the hard wood floor
With her long ... slow
... High heel toe
And the coins in the slots
Know where to go
And she looks like a movie
And she sounds like a star
Then she stops at your window

Puts her foot in the air
Rests a heel on your wall
And you can't help but stare
And she likes how you look
And her eyes say it all
And you come like a sailor
And she smiles coz she knows
And your window fogs up
And your curtain is closed
And all you can hear is
The sound of those shoes
And her long ... slow
... High heel toe
On the hard wood floor
All satisfied ...
As she goes

Hate

Carried
Hard heavy
Long black sack
White nylon noose
Digs in
Hurts
Hung tight
Grip relaxes
Releases
Dumb thud
Useless corpse
Unfeeling
Staring back
Blindly
Pain goes
Grimace follows
Fingers flex
Pink sorrow
Marks fade
Brute bag dragged
Somewhere else
A corner
Propped up proud
Cold wall witness
Alone for now
Until the return
Bastard smirking
Torn mouth
Cavity eyes
Hunched darkly
Madly twisted

Victims' shuffle
Haunting shadow
Afraid to go

Heavenly Scent

Oh, inhale, hold it
Your smell & taste
I've got lucky fingers
And a well-travelled tongue
Your cat's out roaming
Curious, wet & hungry
I'm a scary beast
Prowling manic menace
Down dirty dark alleys
Bat wing trench coat
Iron bar greased
Hairy hands ready
To pry & plunge
My buxom booty

He Fucked Me

I liked the way he looked at me
And fucked me with his eyes
I liked the way he spanked me
And licked inside my thighs

I trusted him completely
Enough to lower my guard
I frogged my legs around him
He fucked me deep and hard

He fucked me in the water
He fucked me on the shore
He fucked me til I came
And then he fucked me more

Love wasn't what I wanted
I let him know the score
So he fucked me up the arse
I was his little whore

Hide and Seek

Here I am
In my mind
Again
Still

And you're here
With me
Again
Still

I'm hiding
From you
With you
Again
Still

Count to ten
Maybe eleven
One more minute
With you
Again
Still

Did you find me?
I'm a good hider
Not as good as you
I can't find you
Again
Still

He Fucked Me

I liked the way he looked at me
And fucked me with his eyes
I liked the way he spanked me
And licked inside my thighs

I trusted him completely
Enough to lower my guard
I frogged my legs around him
He fucked me deep and hard

He fucked me in the water
He fucked me on the shore
He fucked me til I came
And then he fucked me more

Love wasn't what I wanted
I let him know the score
So he fucked me up the arse
I was his little whore

Hide and Seek

Here I am
In my mind
Again
Still

And you're here
With me
Again
Still

I'm hiding
From you
With you
Again
Still

Count to ten
Maybe eleven
One more minute
With you
Again
Still

Did you find me?
I'm a good hider
Not as good as you
I can't find you
Again
Still

How to Spot a Pervert

We are masters and mistresses of disguise, and most adept at looking normal.
We have excellent eyesight, might still wear glasses, and may or may not have mentally undressed you, while looking you straight in the eyes and without you knowing.
We are highly fashion conscious, and dress so badly we neither make statements nor try to be ahead of our time.
We are experts in the bedroom; however this only applies to the subtle moving and positioning of furniture.
We are great lovers of food and can cook, eat and drink, all in the one kitchen; but we are not gastronomes - that would be showing off.
We prefer our own cars to buses and trains. In our own cars we can pick our noses in private.
We know about art, including films, music and painting, but we don't always get it.
We are inherently lazy creatures, and prefer watching TV and sleeping to anything else.
We like libraries, because the books are usually quiet.
We detest public toilets - they are impossible to find and inevitably by the time we get there, we have a new traumatic experience to share with our psychologists.
We have families and friends who we don't really know and who don't really know us, and that's probably just as well.

We are incredibly shallow people with deep thoughts, strong hearts and weak minds.
We are natural cowards who go places we shouldn't and feel more than we should.
We are not nice, but those closest to us think we are. Fools – at least we share that in common.
We aim to be strange, but not different, and often just settle for weird.
We are everybody and we are nobody, except for those times when we're somebody in between.
We are actually impossible to find, unless you're one of us too.

I do I am

I snore I lust
I dream I rust
I fart I laugh

I eat I need
I drink I joke
I smoke I think

I read I piss
I write I shit
I spew I doubt

I love I live
I hate I lie
I fuck I die

I work I look
I bleed I touch
I fight I stay

In and Out

Needle goes in
Blood comes out
Hit goes in
Pain comes out

Rush comes in
Tide goes out
Days come in
Nights go out

Love walks in
Hate crawls out
Hate crawls in
Love walks out

Thirst creeps in
Hunger goes out
Worst creeps in
Best goes out

Cash comes in
Cash goes out
Bills pile up
Stash runs out

Users lob in
Dealers sell out
Family climbs in
Clock chimes out

Needle goes in

Blood comes out
Hit goes in
Pain comes out

Rush comes in
Tide goes out
Days come in
Nights go out

Dreams fly in
Dreams fly out
Debts add up
Time runs out

Collectors come in
Guns come out
Bullets go in
Blood runs out

Cold creeps in
Warmth seeps out
Fear sets in
Lights go out

Air comes in
Breath goes out
Death comes in
Soul gets out

Needle goes in
Blood comes out
Hit goes in
Pain comes out

Rush comes in
Tide goes out
Days come in
Nights go out

In Hoboken

They'd been pokin'
Roun' Hoboken
Hopin' for
Some hillbilly grass

The locals jokin'
In Hoboken
'Bout them chokin'
An' fallin' on their ass

Few words were spoken
In Hoboken
An' they were tokin'
On fine hillbilly grass

Then they were chokin'
In Hoboken
Floatin'
Off their white lilly ass

The locals jokin'
In Hoboken
'Bout them smokin'
An' chokin' on their grass

Their drought was brokin'
In Hoboken
With rain Soakin'
An' runnin' down the glass

Coz they were smokin'

In Hoboken
An' they were tokin'
On fine hillbilly grass

All were jokin'
In Hoboken
Bout' the chokin'
An' floatin' off their ass

They were smokin'
In Hoboken
An' tokin'
On hillbilly grass

Yeah they were smokin'
In Hoboken
Tokin'
On fine hillbilly grass

Manifesto for a Nice Life

Smoke the roach
Right to the end
Burn your fingers
A little

Think sometimes
Of the long run
But laugh now
Whenever you can

Drink plenty of red
Even when you realise
You'll have to pay for it
One way or another

Break a few
Less important rules
But know exactly
What you're doing

Eat well often
If you can afford to
But don't make a living
Out of it

Watch leaves dance
Write crazy thoughts
Talk to animals and
Humans if you must

Sleep with at least

One light on and
A sharp knife
Close by

Metapsychosis

The grub emerges
Slowly
Struggling
With wings
Of some sort
The goo dries
A flame beckons
Like a belly dancer
Her name is fate
My magic carpet circles
Eyes fixed firmly
On the prize
Closer
Closer still
Her flames
Breathe me in
Ah...
Paradise!

Mount Me

I get so hot
Then I cool
I sleep & erupt
I spew ash
Rumble & grumble
Where's my virgin?

I burn deep
Within my molten core
I'm high & I'm low
I'm everything in between
I'm beauty & I'm horror
Where's my virgin?

I smoke & bleed
I'm old & I'll die
I'm my own grave
One day I'll be a giant lake
I am your volcano
Will you be my virgin?

Murphy

Murphy!
Where's my book?
You know the one
I lent you that night
After that day
We met for coffee
I was hung over
Like a madman
You all cute
With your blouse
Unbuttoned
Showing off
Your little brown bra
You noticed me
Looking
So you
Buttoned up
I ate
And we talked
And you
Sure did
Fill out those jeans
So nicely
And we both
Found out
We have much
In common
Both crazy
And writers
Both taken
But open

You smart
As hell
I old
You young
Both wanting
Something
And I still want
My fucking book!

My Angel

If she's an angel
Then she can't stay too long
She has to go back
With a body
And not just anybody
If she's my angel
Then it's my body
That's why she's killing me
It's nothing personal
She's just doing her job

My Brother the Poet

And the waters he walked on
Were puddles
And the best he could do
Was turn wine into piss
And his loaves and fishes
Were from the supermarket
On special
And his three wise men
Were a drunk, a thief
And a murderer
And his disciples
Were sycophants
And his cross
Was a corkscrew
And his rock was rolled
By someone else
Because he was too lazy
And his resurrection
Was only in his mind
When he got high
And he was another narcissist
And he was just like me
And he was nothing like me

My Moon White Corpse

Let me lick your wound
Clean your rusty cut
Taste my salty tongue
On your still moist mound
Curing your wild wet ham
Let me quietly kiss you
Like a secret confessional
I bless your innocence
And sprinkle upon you
A hail of holy water
To wash away the sins
Those callous calling cards
Of stupid stabbing pricks
Now rest and slowly drift
Away in never ending sleep
I have many souls to catch
So your honour I may keep

Not for Love

I wallow
In Germanic daze
Grip my misogyny
With tempered lust
And remember you
Seated back to me
Thin in your dress
I see an outline
High on your hips
Your cheeks smile
Firm and hungry
I cannot see
But know
Your pert pink breasts
Pointing away
I want you
Not for love
I desire one thing
Your soiled panties
To sniff and taste
While I wank
Hard and fast
Over your image
In my dirty mind
I sit on your throne
My warm arse
On your porcelain
My bare feet
Cold on your tiles
The bathroom door
Closed tight

You have a window
And I don't care
You like to watch
My pumping fist
The up and down
My soft hand
On a proud cock
My cobra dances
Entranced
By your danger
I can smell you
And see your line
Of glistening white
My tongue tip
Absorbs your salt
My nose inhales
Your musky stench
You are in me
And we are one
I see you flawless
Pure intoxicating
You poison my blood
Pollute my soul
Your wild discharge
Flows through me
I will have release
On your sealed floor
So you can see
Those clouds of cum
My buckets of joy
That sorry mess
I must clean up
With your cotton

And wash in blue
To kill my sins
And deny you
I wring it dry
But lie again
They're still damp
I hang them out
Put myself back
And flush away
More filth
Wet the tap
And quietly leave
Like it was nothing
But a prison smile
Without pardon
No need for parole
Because it was nothing
A sad mad fantasy
Entirely meaningless
Don't get it wrong
There's no disrespect
Just what it was
A precious moment
Fine filled lunacy
A possible dream
A dark fiction
But maybe not
Some of it's real
As real as words
Cast out scattered
Seeds on a page

Not That Drunk

I'm not that drunk
I'm not that drunk
I'm not that drunk

The air seems solid
It's back to front
The air seems solid

Got all this junk
But not your forehead
Got all this junk

The air seems solid
Two cars out front
But not your forehead

I'm out to lunch
The food is horrid
I'm out to lunch

The food is horrid
I saw the punch
I saw it coming

I didn't flinch
I saw it coming
I'm not that drunk

Not the One

I'm the one
Your mothers warned you about
The one they loved
Before the one who would stay

I'm the one
Your friends say
Is no good for you
But might be ok for them

I'm the one
With all the problems
Maybe even more
Than you

I'm the one
Who would ride a white horse
And save you
If I weren't allergic

I'm the one
Who might commit
All kinds of crimes
Except adultery

I'm the one
Who takes my medicine
In regular small doses
But is never cured

I'm the one

Who is not the one
But just one of many
And happy to be no-one

I'm the one
With something to say
And nowhere to say it
But I do anyway

Ode to a Dirty Old Man

Bukowski
Sat and read poetry
He also sat
When he wrote it
He was never young
Bukowski

He hit life hard
Like his father's beltings
With German efficiency
And the lust
Of a wild Barbarian
Bukowski

Not like Hemingway
And his boorish
Macho bullshit
Nor Rumsfeld who
Also stood at his desk
Adding his Neo-Con shekels

No
Hank was his own man
He called a fuck a fuck
And a phony a phony
He looked a mess but
His conscience was neat

I could be wrong
I didn't know him
Hell his words only

Gave me a glimpse
But what I saw was
Goodness and honour

That beautiful ugly man
Filled with raw honesty
Unafraid to bleed
From his guts free
Down but never out
Bukowski

Ode to a Girl with Perfect Lips

Half a kiss from those full lips
Why did I have to go?
Because it was late
And the morning sun
Was up and waiting

I couldn't work
I couldn't think
My mind was yours
Developing photos
In dark red light
Secretly in my room

When I saw you next
In the bar alone
You ignored me so well
It hurt but I liked it
Not knowing why
But it seemed right

Then the next time
You were fine again
Clear skinned eyes bright
Smile like a dream
And half a kiss
From those full lips

Oh yes
Half a kiss
And those full lips

Oh You Know …

Just rusting with my ever maddening locks
Secretly inside-outing odd and stripy socks
Catching short but cleverly deepening sighs
Fishing in whirling eddies of wonder whys

Unravelling coils in a slow and seeping melt
Feckless flow of words to go wily but misspelt
Unfurled undone unzipped and tripped to fall
Conditioned to slide denied my splatter scrawl

One More Time

I walk alone
Talk to no-one
On my own
Again

Fear the phone
Hear the moan
Silent tone
Again

See the clone
Seed I've sown
Pointed bone
Again

Tip the throne
Smoke a cone
Leave the zone
Again

Outside Out

I'm the lunch stain
On your paper
I'm the button
Off your shirt

At times
I'm like a gas
Invisible
And inert

I'm the quiet one
In the corner
I'm the loner
On the edge

The outsider
Among outsiders
The jumper
On the ledge

Pink

Cheeks pink
Skin soft
Lick tongue
Sweet sticky
Lips dangle

Please Sir

The slow motion farce
It has me by the throat
All those mindless forms
Closed door meetings
Endless ego displays
The silent sounds
Of crushed dignities
The haunted hallways
Change your mind
There's a form for that
Prisoners lunatics
The guards the wardens
The sold souls
Waiting for their super
Hoping for an easy buy back
Three more hoops
To jump through
Before my day is done
Two more attentions
To stand to
Before I can
See the sun
May I skip
To the loo
My darling
Before I come undone
I breathe
My flexible quota
All fully approved
Of course
Permission to go

And quietly die sir
Oh yes
Three more forms
In triplicate
Sick leave
Doctor's note
Another form
Phlegm sample attached
My toilet
My escape
My stinking
Shangrila of peace
The exhaust fan
Sucks out the stench
I wish it could
Take me too

Poetry Court

You are hereby accused
Of crimes against poetry
How do you plead?
Not guilty you say?
Let us hear the evidence
Did you or did you not
Wilfully and recklessly
On more than one occasion
Resort to rhyming couplets
And is it true or false
That you did knowingly
Use that word - 'love'
And try to deny if you will
That you showed complete
And utter disregard for
The laws of modernism
By negligently and with
Malice, fail to mention
Or even allude to one
Myth or mythical character
And to make matters worse
Not a whiff of a canto
No numbered stanzas
And you had the audacity
To fail to mitigate your crimes
With the simple inclusion
Of your middle initial
When signing your name
But it does not stop there
Where in your, so called
Poetry, are the indigenous

Or the icons of our landscape
I'll tell you where they are
Nowhere! Yes, that's right
Not a skerrick, and furthermore
No redeeming references
To either the greats of
Literature or for that matter
Any sign of light hearted
Condescension of our
Beloved minorities
In particular the Semites
And the homosexuals
Guilty I say
Guilty
Guilty

Proust

Breathe in
Breathe out
Blink
Breathe in
Breathe out
Blink
Breathe in
Breathe out
Scratch
Blink
Breathe in
Breathe out
Blink
Fart
Hold breath
Exhale
Die

Shadow Boxer

My mind dances
Its own steps
Old dances
In a new way
Unremembered
But felt
To the death
Thorns in mouth
And blood
Sweeter
And dryer
Than wine
I eat life
Like a stranger
And sleep
The good sleep
Of a man
Satisfied

Sweet Rain

There was a time
When every poem
Was a love song
And every word
Tasted of you

Where hands held
Warm thoughts
And fingers touched
And twirled
Like ballerinas

There was a time
When you were
My reason
And you were
My rhyme

When your spring
Was my season
And my winter
Went all but blind

Such a time
Full of flowers
Full of sunshine
And never enough
Precious hours

To be with you
Like long hot showers

On icy mornings
And steamy breaths
That say I do

Those days are gone
Too soon too few
No tunes no colours
No me no you

And though my days
Grow shorter too
A desert greens
From your sweet rain

My memories
Of you

Ten Past Four

The screeching of the saw
The leeching of the whore
Short-lived vows we swore
Our holy hearts we tore

Life's simple joy no more
Playing dress-ups in the store
The warming wool we wore
Watching ships from shore

The clouds within that pour
The never healing sore
The constant search for more
Those rules that break the law

The never being sure
Not knowing what life's for
Now or then or nevermore
The time was ten past four

The Lady and Me

We met long ago
In a previous life
The lady and me
When she was a cat
And I was a flea

I was her itch
And she was my scratch
The lady and me
When she was a cat
And I was a flea

Sometimes she'd let me
Sleep in her fur
So soft a bed
The tick of her heart
The lick of her purr

Sometimes she'd let me
Drink from her milk
From her special dish
Me just a pest
With her wrapped in silk

We were so happy
Such an odd pair
A fat little flea
And his feline queen
Her tail in the air

Those were the days

In that previous life
The lady and me
I lived like a king
Like she was my wife

Now I'm long gone
For I was a flea
And she lived on
For she was a cat
Quite unlike me

Sometimes I wonder
If she can see
In her dreams
When she scratches
Her fat little flea

So long ago
In that previous life
The lady and me
When she was my cat
And I was her flea

The Princess and the Lune

I creep in
And linger
Awkwardly
In the doorway
And eventually
Sit between
Kurt and Lover Boy
And my meal for three
Comes with beer
And fries
And salad
And I eat
And offer
And share
And Kurt eats
And Lover Boy doesn't
And the princess
Is tall and thin
Smart as hell
But hates men
And dreams
Impossibly
Of respect
For her mind
So beautiful
And Kurt says
Isn't she great?
And I say nothing
But think
I'd rather look
At her

Than listen
To all that feminist crap
And my ego
Sinks back into its hole
And I clap
With good manners
The enlightened
With the mad
And the waitress
Exudes life
Like I remember
From years ago
And my mind
Wants to tip her
And my groin
Wants to whip her
And Kurt finishes our meal
And Lover Boy feigns disdain
And I clap on
Like a priest
In an orgy
Of nuns

The Stains

Her stains
Have become mine
And I needed them
Like I needed her
Not to keep her
But to remember
The stains
And know
How it feels

The Very Last

I'll give you all
But my very last
I'll keep that
Just for me
And them

All those ones
Parts of twos
And threes
Of love
The multiplier

You deserve all
Except that
My very last
Too much burden
For anyone

Toast-Masters

Here's to the power elite
The godfathers
And godmothers of poetry

Here's to the editors
The arbiters of taste
Who make and break poets

Here's to the hand-wringers
The psychological castrators
The networkers and cronies

Here's to the sycophants
The suck holes and sell-outs
All the hangers on

Here's to the publishers
The politically correct
And all the tripe they print

Here's to the pretenders
The dead journals
And the benefits of hindsight

Here's to the farcical waste
All those boring books
The ones real people don't read

Here's to the others
The rejected
The unpublished

The unfashionable
The uncompromising
The unaffected

The disconnected
The disenfranchised
The independents

The incorruptible
The anarchists
The heretics

The loners
The questioners
The seekers of truth

The down and out
The powerless
The meek

The strong
The thick skinned
The ones who never give up!

Senryu

a church
next to a pub
worshippers gather

Australian made
even the defects
are patriotic

death –
the winner
finishes last

fakebook
falsebook
farcebook

poets
are aliens
with cameras

the neighbours
putting rubbish in my bin
should I be envious

twits tweeting
oh fuck –
alliteration

wank words -
steep learning curve
absolutely

Thanks

For my great loves: books, drugs, food, movies, music, porn, sleep and television.

www.ingramcontent.com/pod-product-compliance
Lightning Source LLC
Chambersburg PA
CBHW061506040426
42450CB00008B/1498